Graeme Base:
Writer and Illustrator

Interviewed by Eleanor Curtain
Photography by Ross Tonkin

I'm Graeme Base, and I'm a writer and
an illustrator. I live in Melbourne, Australia,
with my wife and children. My books are
sold in many countries all over the world.

People often ask me how I became an illustrator.

I used to draw and write at school, and I wrote my first book when I was eight years old. It was a "Book of Monsters." I did all of the illustrations in colored pencil, but I didn't get it published!

After I left school, I studied art and design. Eventually I began illustrating children's books that other people had written. I often wanted to make changes to the stories to make the words and pictures work better. And so I decided to write and illustrate my own stories.

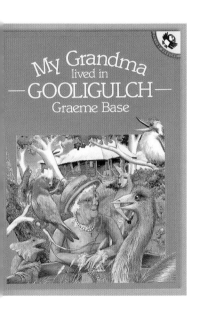

My Grandma Lived in Gooligulch was my first published book.

It's hard to say where my ideas come from.

They often arrive just when I'm in the middle of something, and it's very important that the ideas don't get away. I always write them down or draw a picture of them as soon as possible.

Mostly I love to draw animals. My stories are about fantastic things and events. They aren't real, but I use real animals as a reference to make the fantasy more convincing.

My first really successful book was *Animalia*. I wanted to illustrate as many animals as I could. I also wanted to make a book with lots and lots of detail and things to discover. This was the kind of book I enjoyed as a child.

I wrote *Animalia* using alliteration. That's when most of the words on a page begin with the same letter or sound. I thought a book like that would be a lot of fun for people to read aloud.

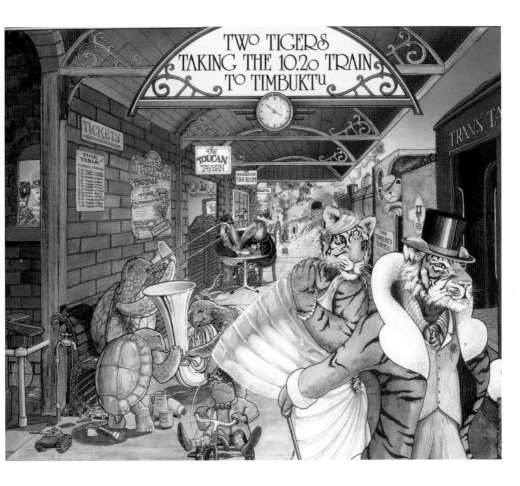

I put the little boy in every picture to make people look closely at the pictures, rather than rushing through the pages. (It's really a picture of me when I was young!)

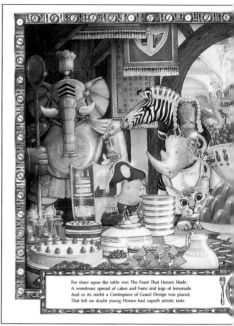

For there upon the table was The Feast That Horace Made,
A wondrous spread of cakes and buns and jugs of lemonade.
And in its midst a Centrepiece of Grand Design was placed,
That left no doubt young Horace had superb artistic taste.

I have written several other books.
When I wrote *The Eleventh Hour*, I thought
of the title first. I knew I wanted to write
a mystery story, with the clues hidden in
the artwork. Everything in the story is
based around the number 11. Everything
would happen at 11 o'clock.

But if the Guests had hoped to eat the Banquet there and then,
They soon found out their Host had plans for what they'd eat and when,
For Horace told them firmly not a crumb would they devour,
Until the time that he had set – THE ELEVENTH HOUR.

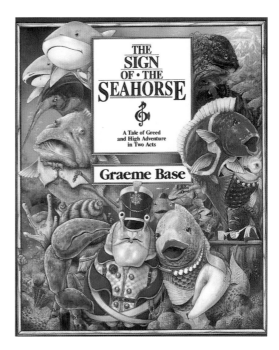

THE
SIGN
OF · THE
SEAHORSE

A Tale of Greed
and High Adventure
in Two Acts

Graeme Base

The picture that took the longest to create was the feast. All of that food took a very long time to get right!

The Sign of the Seahorse was inspired by my first scuba diving experience.

I work in a studio at the top of my house. It has lots of windows because I need very good light.

I prefer drawing to writing. In fact, I really began writing books so that I could have the fun of illustrating them!

At some stage, I start to scribble. When I get the image that I want, and I know what I want to do, I plan the illustrations in detail.

My paintings are done on illustration board with watercolors and transparent inks. I use brushes, pencils, technical drawing pens, and a scalpel (for scratching).

I also use a special tool called an airbrush, which sprays colors onto the board. It is very handy. It helps me paint skies and mist and breath from horses' mouths!

For *The Worst Band in the Universe,* I made a small clay model of each character to see what it would look like.

Then I made a larger model, also of clay. I made a plaster cast of this, and I filled it with latex and foam so it could be stretched and moved.

After I made the models, I could move them into any position I wanted and then draw them. I could also photograph the models and scan them into my computer.

Sometime in the future, I would like to illustrate a whole book on my computer.

My only real hobby is playing music. Whenever I need a break from illustrating books, I pick up the guitar or play the piano. I'd love to work as a musician!

I write a lot of music on the guitar and on keyboards. I hope one day to make a record or maybe even write the music score for a movie.

Books by Graeme Base

1983   *My Grandma Lived in Gooligulch*
1986   *Animalia*
1988   *The Eleventh Hour*
1992   *The Sign of the Seahorse*
1996   *The Discovery of Dragons*
1999   *The Worst Band in the Universe*